DEDICATION

This book is dedicated to my loves, Easton, Alana, and Eddie – plus all
the other military children and families. Your lives are turned upside-down
and inside-out with military movement, being raised in a world of constant
change and wonder. Easton and Alana – you may not be able to verbalize
yet what sacrifice means, however, you embody it every day we cannot
be stationed together as a family. Eddie – you have truly grown into an
outstanding young man. I could not be prouder, and I love you all!

To my military spouse – your love and support across thousands of miles
has made being stationed apart for over two years survivable (and hopefully
ending soon for our family's sake). I love you and couldn't imagine doing
this journey with anyone else.

Also, I'd be remiss if I left out my family and friends – I cherish your support
and ongoing friendships.

MY MOMMY IS A
HERO
IN UNIFORM

By: AnnMarie Puttbrese

Copyright © 2017 AnnMarie Puttbrese
Illustrations: Gau Family Studios // Design: Megan Costik
Printed by CreateSpace

ISBN-13: 978-0997882414
ISBN-10: 0997882417

INSPIRATION FROM MY HEROES

Easton - Age 5

Alana - Age 3

Today is the day
I say good-night,

To my mommy by phone
or computer light.

But why, might you ask, must this be so?
I'll tell you my story, it's special, you know.

For my mommy is far, far away,
Spending time saving good guys, day after day.

What objects do you
see in this picture?

She flies by
helicopters,
planes, or jets,

To protect you
and me from
strangers we
have not met.

What color is the helicopter?

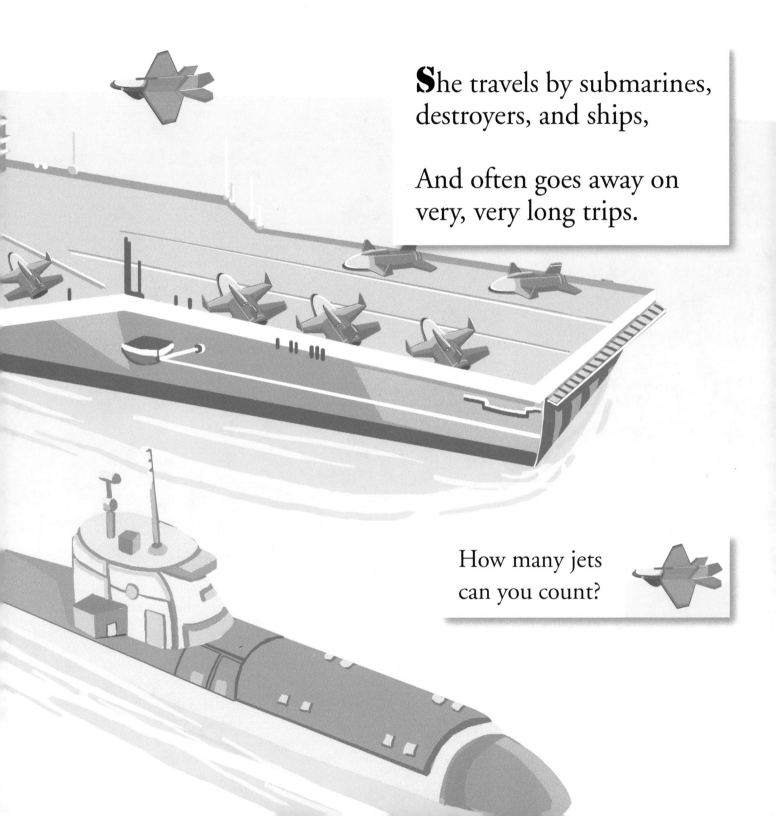

She travels by submarines, destroyers, and ships,

And often goes away on very, very long trips.

How many jets can you count?

She hikes through forests, sand, and rocky mountain tops,

To get a good view from the perfect spot.

How many military women can you count?

She moves by tanks, trucks, and jeeps,

Crossing hills and valleys that may be steep, or slightly deep.

How many wheels can you count?

She may even march, ruck, or crawl,

Being ever so careful not to fall.

What do you think they have in their backpacks?

She cares for the sick, wounded, and those in danger,

To fix them up, and keep them safe from strangers.

What colors can you see on the helicopter?

Her job can be thankless and sometimes scary,

But she stands bravely to help the friendly military.

How many firefighters can you see?

She is my hero,
I cherish her so,

My love for her just
grows and grows.

She is so special, so special you see,

Because she fights for our freedom, to protect you and me.

How many hearts can you count?

What objects do you see in the sand?

I am so lucky, so lucky indeed,

For my mommy helps keep our land freed.

I am so special,
so special it's true,

Because I am, and always
will be, her hero too!

WELCOME HOME
MOMMY

Is your mommy your hero, too?

The Puttbrese Family

CPSIA information can be obtained
at www.ICGtesting.com
Printed in the USA
LVHW072312220319
611620LV00002B/5/P